The Village of Malvern Wells

as it was in the 1940's

During & just after the 2nd World War

This record of the village of Malvern Wells, as it was in the 1940's, is **dedicated to my cousin *Lil Roberts*** who gave me the inspiration to write it. Lil lived her entire life in the village. Sadly she died there in January 2010.

The Village of Malvern Wells
Ray Roberts
Published by Aspect Design 2011
Malvern, Worcestershire, United Kingdom.
Printed by Aspect Design
89 Newtown Road, Malvern, Worcs. WR14 1PD
United Kingdom
Tel: 01684 561567
E-mail: books@aspect-design.net
Website: www.aspect-design.net

All Rights Reserved.
Copyright © 2011 Ray Roberts

Ray Roberts has asserted his moral right
to be identified as the author of this work.

The right of Ray Roberts to be identified as the author of this work has been asserted in accordance with Section 77 of the Copyright, Designs and Patents Act 1988.

This book is sold subject to the condition that it shall not, by way of trade or otherwise, be lent, resold, hired out or otherwise circulated without the publisher's prior consent in any form of binding or cover other than that in which it is published and without a similar condition including this condition being imposed on the subsequent purchaser.

A copy of this book has been deposited with the British Library Board

Cover Design Copyright © 2011 Aspect Design
Original photograph Copyright © Ray Roberts

ISBN 978-1-905795-84-0

The Village of Malvern Wells

*as it was in the 1940s -
during and just after the 2nd World War*

Ray Roberts

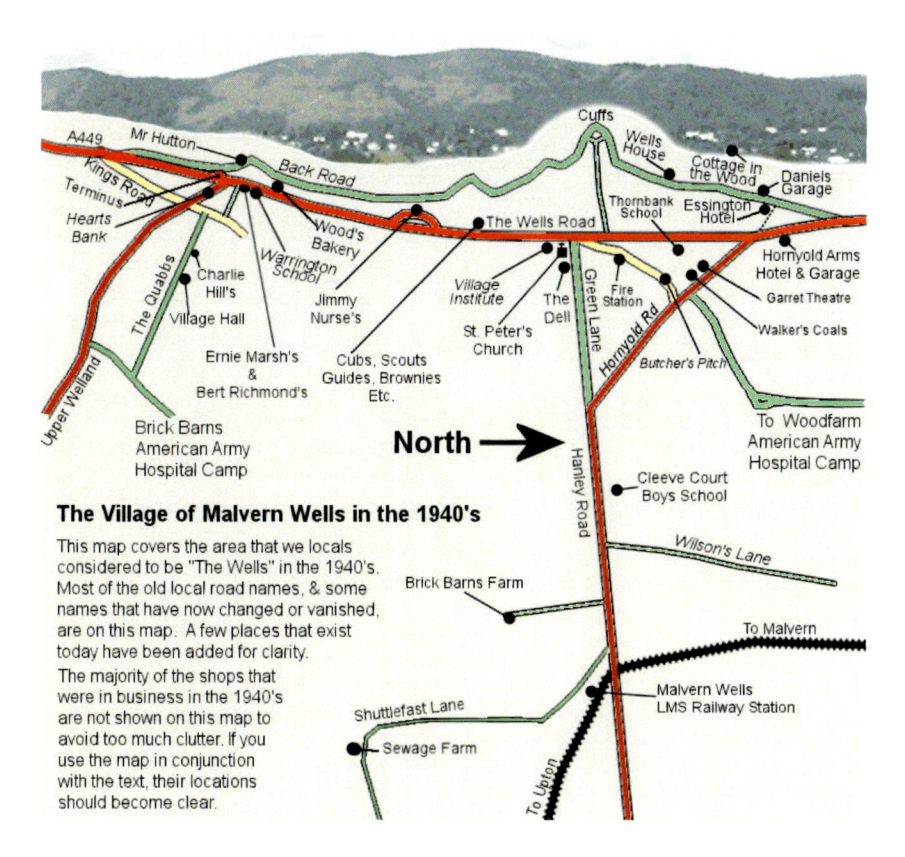

Malvern Wells in the 1940's

The Village of Malvern Wells in the 1940's

This map covers the area that we locals considered to be "The Wells" in the 1940's. Most of the old local road names, & some names that have now changed or vanished, are on this map. A few places that exist today have been added for clarity.

The majority of the shops that were in business in the 1940's are not shown on this map to avoid too much clutter. If you use the map in conjunction with the text, their locations should become clear.

This shows the area that we locals considered "The Wells" in the 1940's. The street names above are the ones we used, as children, at that time

Introduction

This is mainly my personal recollections together with the recollections of old friends who all grew up in the Wells with me. Each friend has confirmed or revived old memories, they have also reminded me of some missing detail(s) or recalled a long forgotten name. We all agree that Malvern Wells was then considered to be the area roughly bounded to the North from the Holywell Road junction with Wells Road., down to the (Hanley Road) LMS Railway Station. The Southern boundary was from the Bus Terminus down to Assarts Lane. The Hills forming the Westerly boundary.   It was just known as "The Wells" and was blessed with many shops, businesses, schools & services. They ensured plenty of local employment for the villagers. There was a real community spirit and everybody seemed to know everybody else.

I was born between the two World Wars in a small 2 up, 2 down, end terrace cottage "down the Quabbs" (Assarts Road). We had gas light, mains water & outside toilet. The "bathroom" was a tin bath in front of the fire!

When I was about 5 we moved to Green Lane. There we had inside toilet & bathroom with mains water (no hot water). We still only had gaslight until my dad paid for "The electricity" to be put in!   I lived there until I married in the mid-1950s.

My first school was **Warrington C of E School**. At about 11 my parents sent me to Lyttleton Prep & Choir School in Gt Malvern until it closed in the mid-40s. I then spent about 12 months at the Wyche School. The Headmaster, Percy Stains, was the best teacher I ever had! I then passed for the Technical School in Worcester. On leaving School I worked for AERE (Atomic Energy Research Establishment) at The Lees, Thirlstane Road. When AERE moved to Harwell I then transferred to TRE (The Telecommunication Research Establishment) until I Joined the RAF.

My cousin Lil Roberts started me on this project following a chat we had at her 80th birthday party. She told me that several years ago, just before her husband Gordon (my cousin) died, he contacted somebody who wished to know some local village history. Gordon started to relate his recollections only to be told that they must be false memories as the Wells was never like that. The "researcher" was not interested in what Gordon had to say. We decided that an accurate record must be made whilst the people who lived at that time were still alive and able to confirm the details. Lil & myself started a list there and then, it has been expanded and added to many times since then. Sadly Lil died about 2 ½ years later, giving me a renewed urgency to complete of this record.

I will generally use the names we used as children for roads etc. throughout this booklet, with the "Official" names in brackets. The reason we always used these "local" names may be partly explained by recalling that all street names & direction signs were removed or obliterated in 1939, at the start of the war, to make life difficult for the enemy in the event of an invasion.

I have written this as a tour, starting near to where I was born "Down **The Quabbs**" (Assarts Road), going roughly clockwise.

Ray Roberts

ray.roberts@malvern-hills.co.uk

Malvern Wells in the 1940's

During and just after the 2nd World War

Opposite what is now Heathlands Close, was probably the smallest **Public Hall** in the country. The stage was so small that only a few people could get on to it at the same time. Many front rooms would be much larger that the hall. It is now converted into a much larger house. I went there with the Cubs to practice for a concert but it was too small to be of any use.

Now just known as "The Hall"

A little further up the road was **Charlie Hill's** general grocery stores. This tiny shop was really just a large shed & had previously been run by a Mr Edwards.

A regular Double Decker Bus Service, the **144**, ran from Birmingham, to & from the Wells, every 20 minutes throughout the day. On the Wells Road (A449) a few hundred yards inside the 30 MPH speed limit signs there still is the **Bus Terminus**. The Terminus is the large semi-circular area cut into the side of the hill, lined with a high Malvern Stone wall, it was built for the buses to turn in. The buses could not turn there in one go, the conductress (it was usually "conductresses", men were still in the armed services) would see the bus reverse back across the Wells Road, controlling the traffic and signaling to the bus driver with a whistle! The driver and

Bus terminus on the left, Bus Shelter & old fire station building on the right

conductor then had a 20 minute rest at the terminus, leaving for Birmingham as the next bus arrived from there. A child's return ticket to Malvern was a 2 ¼ d. return, pronounced "Tuppenny farthing" - slightly less than one penny today. During the late evening the buses only went between the Wells and the Malvern Link bus station - then along Spring Lane.

The bus shelter is still opposite the Bus Terminus, until recently **Public Toilets** were below the **Bus Shelter**. They were finally closed due to mis-use.

By the North side of the Shelter was a very small "**Fire Station**" which contained only a Hand-Cart type Fire Engine.

Above the terminus, a little way along Top Road, sometimes called Back Road or even Upper Road (Holy Well Road) **Mr Hutton** had a little business recharging radio accumulators.

Just down Hearts Bank (Upper Welland Road) on the left, **Mrs Wood** supplied bus drivers, conductors and conductresses with cups of tea.

Back Road

At the top of Hearts Bank **Willis Hill** cut hair for 6d in a little shed behind his house.

About 60 yards along the Wells Road was Ernie **Marsh's General Stores.** I recall that Marsh's sold Ice cream just after the war, quite a luxury then. More recently the shop was known as the Top-Shop & at the time of writing, is a computer shop called Microprice. Ernie's brother, **Walter Marsh**, was a well known & popular local councillor & had been Chairman of the MUDC (Malvern Urban District Council)

Marsh's right. Bert Richmond's, center. Then Warrington School

Ron Jones & Charlie Hannable repaired shoes in Marsh's rear room.

In the adjoining next door shop **Bert Richmond** was an Ironmonger & Blacksmith, he sold paraffin, rabbit nets & wires, rabbit skins, hardware/Ironmongery, chickens, etc   That part of the building has now disappeared completely. Bert also had a Blacksmiths yard behind his shop with the entrance just down "Blacksmith's Pitch" or "Richmond Bank" (it is remembered by both names for obvious reasons), the narrow road down the side of Marsh's shop (now Microprice).   I vividly recall that the shop always smelled strongly of the paraffin that had soaked into the floor from spills when filling customers containers.

At the bottom of Richmond Bank was a small tea shop, also used by the bus men and women.

Just up the bank past the tea room was a small shed that I understand was the original bakery of Stanley Wood, who had the bakery a few hundred yards further along the Main Road (see next page).

The school next door to Richmonds was then known as **Warrington Church of England School**, although usually just called **"The Wells School"** The inscription is still over the main entrance keeping alive the connection with "**Eliza Warrington**" who lived at the Belvedere, a house just up the road on the opposite side. The headmaster was "Boss" Watson, Mrs Hatfield was the infant teacher and

Inscription over entrance

Miss Wills taught everybody else with Boss Watson. Many local children spent their entire schooldays there. The other main options for pupils were the Worcester Grammar Schools entrance exam aged about 11 or Worcester Technical School entrance exam at about 13.

Warrington School building today

Stanley Wood's bakery was in the large Malvern Stone House opposite the Abbey School. He baked through the night, delivering during the day in a basket-work hand cart. He later got an "old" Rolls Royce car with a large basket on the drop down boot lid. He delivered whatever the weather! Very tasty bread, (I used to race my mother as to who got the crust). When I was a little older I often helped him deliver bread in his "Rolls".

"The Bakery" as it is today

Just opposite the Bakery was the **Abbey Girls Boarding School**. It was then a private, very high class, school for young ladies! It is still a school but is now known as the Abbey College, catering for international students aged 14 and over..

Next to the Abbey School in a large private house was the **Doctors Surgery of Dr Fuller & Dr Fairley-Clarke** (When they retired, a Dr Blackman took over the practice.

Between the Bakery and the "hump" was the **Police Station** with a resident policemen, PC Halford. There was later a parking spot cut into the garden for the Policeman's Motor-Bike (a water cooled LE Velocette), you can still see the mark in the wall where the cutting was filled in later.

On the middle section of the hump **Jimmy Nurse,** a very old man it seemed to us, had his shop. He had a large white beard and always wore a white apron. Mr Nurse sold biscuits,

"The Old Police Station" today

sweets, cakes, hot pasties, paraffin and repaired bicycles. During the war he was the local stockist for "Harvo" bread. The shop interior was a maze of corridors all made up with empty large biscuit tins. His shop and shop windows were covered with many pre-war posters. All the hand written notices with special offers etc., that he pinned up outside the shop, ended with the words "Nuff Said". When Jimmy Nurse died his shop was rebuilt and became Wardroper's Wet Fish shop.

Next door (Now the Wells Joinery) was a Garage & Petrol Pumps called **"Humphries Automobile & Agricultural Engineers"** The petrol pumps were by the side of the road just up the bank. Humphries also ran a Taxi Service.

Observe the petrol pumps overhanging the roadway

Another building along the road, just past where **Daniels Garage** now is, was a wooden Bungalow used by the **Malvern Wells Scouts, Guides, Brownies & Cubs.** This was next to the small steel framed bungalow of the two Miss Cotterells (visible in picture above).

Now, crossing over the road:

The first large Malvern stone building was **Dawes Grocery** and Green-Grocery. The Dawes family came to Malvern Wells during the War as a result of the heavy bombing in Birmingham. They took over the business from an elderly Mr & Mrs Parker. The Dawes gave a much quicker service than we had been used to in the village, this caused Holbrook's to lose a lot of business. The building has more recently been known as Croque-en-Bouche & now is called "The old Croque B & B"

A much earlier photo of the building

The Building itself was owned by **Miss Brewer**. Miss Brewer was a very well known local lady who lived in the building and gave Piano lessons in a room at the back.

The next red-brick building held several businesses:-

Adams & Melville, left double-front. Chemist, right double-front. Bank, right

The right hand shop window was then a similar window to the one still on the left hand side of the building and contained **Lloyds Bank**. The bank was accessed by the side-entrance door

Bank entrance

The right-hand, double fronted business was **Ron Jeffes Chemist** (Now "Salon 49"). Ron Jeffes also sold wine, cameras, film, projectors, torches, batteries, binoculars, telescopes etc. If he hadn't got it in stock he would try to get it for you. As a schoolboy I also worked part time for 'Mr Jeffes' delivering, helping to wash out dirty (used) medicine bottles in the dispensary & whatever else that he wanted doing.

The last shop in that building (now "Gandolfi") was a WRVS (Women's Royal Voluntary Service) shop during the war but then became **Adams & Melville** S/H junk shop. That end of the building was owned by a Billy Clare.

A room in the next large Malvern Stone Building was used as a Surgery by **Dr Wright**. Dr Wright later moved to Priory Road, Malvern

The next large Malvern stone building before the Village Institute was **Holbrook's Grocery shop.** Holbrook's sold everything you needed for the weekly shop including such variety as bundles of firewood & packets of seed. It was also the village Paper Shop & Post Office. Sometimes in the holidays I would deliver the papers around the Wells and help in the back of

Holbrook's shop building today

the shop. The job I hated the most was turning the coffee roaster. If you slackened off, the coffee burnt, then there was trouble. Much easier but very boring was filling what seemed like hundreds of blue paper bags with (exactly.....never over!) 2 lbs of sugar. For many years it became a private home, then recently it re-opened as a general stores "The 207 Store", with a Boutique in the Post Office half. Sadly "207" was short-lived, however Tailorbird Boutique now uses all the shop space.

Next we come to the **Village Institute,** which was really the centre of village life. There were regular dances, films and other entertainment, as well as Youth Club & Sunday School meetings. Mr Terry was the caretaker at that time. (In the early 60's my mother took on the job of live-in caretaker for the Church and Institute. Together with my then small son I lived there with my mum for some years.)

The Working Mens Club was, and still is, in a room below the Village Institute. It had the first One-Armed-Bandit in the Wells. It is now renamed The Wells Club

The "Village Institute"

The red public **Telephone Box** outside the Institute was the main telephone for most villagers. A red phone box is still there

Next to the Institute was **St Peters Church**, then usually called "The Wells Church", sadly now converted to housing. We had our own Vicar, the Rev. Reece-Jones, (Later the Rev. Milne) who lived at the Vicarage, a large house with extensive grounds, in Hanley Road.

An early photograph of Saint Peters Church

A few yards down Green Lane was, and still is, a hotel called **The Dell.**

Up the drive that is immediately opposite the top of Green Lane, **Mrs Edwards** ran a Guest House called Hartfield.

The bottom of that drive was used as the **144 Midland Red Bus stop.** When coming from Malvern the buses stopped outside Holbrook's shop. To get off the bus there, you asked for a ticket to the "Wells Church".

Walking roughly North East from the top of Green Lane, down

"Butchers Pitch" (Grundy's Lane), the first building you came to on the left was **Chris Leyland's** butchers shop, it was right opposite the Fire Station (yes we also had a fire station). Chris had bought the business off Tom Lee shortly before. For a while I worked for Chris on Saturdays, delivering meat on his delivery bicycle with a basket on the front, making sausages (there was more 'biscuit' than meat in them in those days) as well as scrubbing and cleaning up at the end of the day.

The Wells **Fire Station** was not then manned full time. The firemen were stationed at Gt Malvern Fire Station, a large old building opposite the front of the Abbey Hotel that is now the hotel staff quarters. My dad was an Auxiliary Fireman before the war at the Wells but became a full time Fireman at Great Malvern during the war. The name of the Auxiliary Fire Service (AFS) changing to the National Fire Service (NFS) at the

The Fire Station

commencement of the war. Although I was not aware of it at the time I was very privileged. My father was not called up into the regular services, I believe it was because of an ear problem from which he had always suffered. So I regularly saw him both at home and on visits to the Fire Station.

Malvern Wells Auxiliary Fire Brigade about 1939 (My dad 3rd from Right)

Opposite the Butchers, next to the Fire Station was **Birchley's Builders yard**. It was called Claremont Works. The yard is now a private cul-de-sac and has retained the connection by being named Claremont Court.

Back on the Wells Road just before the first shop there was a very large **Bill Board** advertising that week's Film Shows at the Picture House & The Theatre. At that time the Malvern Theatre was primarily a Picture House, therefore Malvern had two full time picture houses. This meant that one could see 5 full length feature films a week. Only the Picture House opened on a Sunday.

Adjacent to the Bill Board, the first shop on the right, a single room lock-up shop, was **Geoff Roberts** (my dad), Boot and Shoe repairs and sales. Contrary to another "History of the Wells" that I have read, he did not have a trap-door in the floor going down to his workshop. Any trap-door in the floor would have taken him straight into Mr Smith's bake-house below.

Geoff Roberts at his shop

L to R - Gowing's,   Creese's, Richardson's, Smith's,   Geoff Roberts

The next shop was **Smiths Sweet Shop/** Cake Shop/ Tobacconist/ and Cake Bakery. Smiths bake-house was immediately below my dad's shop (dad had no heating bills!). Mrs Smith was a little 'old' lady with a billowing mop of very white hair. She would sell cigarettes to children as long as they promised not to tell their father she had done so. I do have first hand knowledge of this as I bought my first packets of 5 Woodbines off her, however I did have to go round to her back door, after the shop was shut, before she would serve me.

Adjoining Smiths was **Richardson Antiques.** The shop door that was then by the left side of the window has long since disappeared.

Next was **Mr. Creese's** double fronted shop selling haberdashery, shoes, work-clothes, carpet, linoleum etc. Mr Creese's left side window has now been changed to a smaller sash style, similar to the upper floor windows.

Creese's was then a double fronted shop

The last shop in the row was **Miss Gowing's** Shop selling High Class (very expensive) ladies clothing, milliner, hosiery, towels, sheets, etc.

Right opposite Miss Gowing's shop at the top of the steep track, **Cuffs** had their bottling factory at the **Holy Well.** They produced Mineral Water and all sorts of "Pop". Cuffs also gave a regular delivery service all around the area. At about this time my Uncle lived in the cottage at the right-hand side of the main Holy Well building.

The Holy Well

Just past and opposite Miss Gowing's shop is the **War Memorial.** The local Cubs and Scouts together with local people attended the Armistice Day services there during the war. All the service men were, of course, at war.

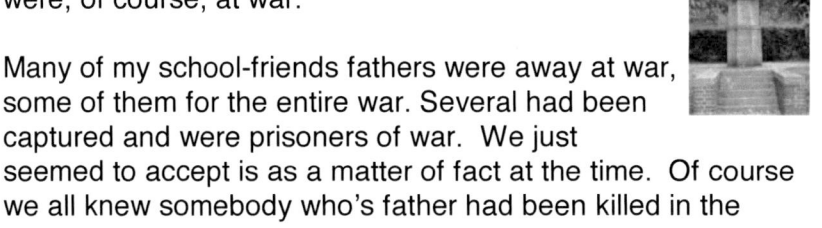

Many of my school-friends fathers were away at war, some of them for the entire war. Several had been captured and were prisoners of war. We just seemed to accept is as a matter of fact at the time. Of course we all knew somebody who's father had been killed in the fighting.

About 50 yards to the North of Miss Gowing's shop was **May Place Hotel**.

Next to May Place, **Mr Pillon** ran his taxi business from home.

A little further on was Miss Rogers **Thornbank School**, another private school for girls. Thornbank took in both day girls and borders, the school uniform colour was a very distinctive grey & purple. Thornbank Cottage, the little Bungalow on the 'inside' corner of Butchers Pitch & Hornyold Road was used by the senior girls.

Thornbank Cottage

The Hornyold Arms Public House (once known as the Admiral Benbow) was very popular during the war with the American soldiers from the local Hospital Camps and then later with the soldiers of all nationalities who used the camps for many years after the war. In an open room on the lower ground floor behind the Hornyold Arms lived a pet Monkey in a cage. Local kids often went round the back to tease the poor animal. There was also a rifle range there. The landlord at that time was Mr Chandler.

The Hornyold Arms

Next to the Hornyold Arms was the Hornyold **Petrol Station & Garage.** The garage business was owned by a **Bert Schneider** who also ran a Taxi business. The garage also charged Wireless Accumulators as most radios used "wet" lead/acid batteries (a "charge" cost 6d and lasted about a week. Most people had three batteries, one on charge, one in use and one on standby.).

Opposite the Hornyold, off Holy Well Road, was the **Essington Hotel** and Bar. The very small bar was very popular with a

The Essington, top left. Hornyold far right. Note in the foreground the road-sweepers cart just before the bus stop.

select group of local regulars. The beer, *Flowers Ale*, was drawn straight from the wood in the cellar. The Essington was owned by Mr Hanson, a local farmer who farmed at Brick Barns Farm just above the LMS Railway Station down Hanley Road.

A short distance further up Holy Well Road **The Cottage in the Wood** Hotel was in business then, and still is today.

About half way between the Essington and Holy Well was the **Wells House School** for boys. The Headmaster was Mr Darvell. The school uniform was bright red jackets, the boys could often be seen walking and playing on the hills above the school. A punishment sometimes used for very naughty boys was often to get Mr Humphries, from the garage in Wells Road, to take the boys a fair way from the school and drop them off to find their own way back. Occasionally he would take pity on the boys and drop them closer to the school. The school was not the most attractive of buildings, however I had mixed feelings seeing it recently being partly demolished for rebuilding. It had always seemed to be a part of the village and could be spotted from miles around. It does seem that the developers will retain its general outline - if it is ever finished!. During the school holidays the Wells House was used as a summer school. Frequently it was used by girls from other parts of the country, this acted as quite a magnet for the local boys.

The Wells House School

Behind the Essington Hotel on the other side of Holy Well Road where Halas House now is, **Bert Daniels** started his

Motor repair Business in 1950. Bert sold my father a very smart second hand Austin 7 Ruby Saloon from there. My dad kept pigs in the **Pig's Cot's** behind Bert's garage.

Going down Hornyold Road (Hanley Road) on the right, behind Gloucester House, Miss Popperwell ran a small theatre called the **Garret Theatre,** giving several shows a year. It was also used as a Marionette theatre.

Just past Gloucester House was **Walker's Coals** office. Everybody had coal fires at that time so Walker's were always very busy. Some time later **Tilt's Coals** took the business over. The small white painted Coal Office building can still be seen flush to the side of the pavement. The slightly set back house adjoining is called "The Coach House".

The Coal Office building

A little further down the road, Walton Villa, on the corner of Butchers Pitch (Grundy's Lane), was the wartime home of **Batsford Books** of London. Batsford had their offices there and stored thousands of books on the premises as well as using many other storage rooms around the area.

George Bullock had a builders yard in the grounds of Walton Villa (this was eventually taken over by a Mr Allen).

The next large old Malvern Stone house on the right going down, was the **Malvern Wells Vicarage**, lived in by the Rev. Reece-Jones, the Vicar of St Peters Church. The extensive gardens were used for various church Garden Parties and such like event.

A large house on the North side of the road was called **Moorlands House**. The owner was a Mr Jones the founder of Windshields of Worcester, Mr. Jones also bred Hereford Cattle very successfully.

On the left further down Hanley Road, and a few hundred yards below Green Lane, was **Cleeve Court School** for Boys. Cleeve Court took in day boys as well as borders.

Cleeve Court Schol buildings today

On the opposite side of the road past Cleeve Court School, **Mrs Rodway** ran a small grocery shop in her house in Shuttlefast Lane.

At the far end of Shuttlefast Lane was the local **Sewage Farm.** The sewage from the Wells and the Wyche was treated there. It consisted of a screen to remove solids followed by three settlement tanks. The water coming out at the end of the treatment was said to be pure enough to drink and went into a local stream.

Further down Hanley Road, just above what is now the Three Counties Showground, was the **LMS** (London, Midland & Scottish) **Railway Station**. Regular trains ran from Gt Malvern, through Upton-upon-Severn & Tewkesbury through to Ashchurch. The "Coffee-pot" engine was affectionately known as the **"Ashchurch Flyer"**. The Station Master was Tim Nice. As with the other railway stations in Malvern, "The Wells" was used during the war to bring in wounded soldiers to the local Hospital Camps.

Malvern Wells LMS Station

There were also several buses a day running between Gt Malvern & Gloucester & Cheltenham (via Hanley Road, Welland & Castlemorton). Locally it was called the **Gloucester Bus,** although some remember it as the **Green Bus** due to its colour, as against the 144 Midland Red.

The American Army Hospital Camps

During World War II the Wells was surrounded by **American Army Hospital Camps**.

Part of the Golf Course was taken over as **Woodfarm Camp** and the field known as 40 Acres at the bottom of the Quabbs (Assarts Road) became **Brick Barns Camp.**

There were also two camps at **Blackmore** and one at **Merebrook**.

When the Americans left, some the camps were taken over for a while to house DP's (Displaced Persons) of all nationalities.

For a very short while after the war, Brick Barns was used to house **German PoW's** (Prisoners of War) followed by a great many DP's, however it reportedly was forced to shut down the DP camp as a result of complaints from the Abbey Girls School about the behaviour of some of the inmates.

After that the camps were used by various British army units until they were all finally abandoned.

Woodfarm camp became military billets for some years and is now a modern housing estate.

Brick Barns lasted the longest as it became St Wulstan's **TB hospital** and then a **mental rehabilitation** hospital until the mid 1970's. It is now a modern housing development and a Nature Reserve

Summary

During much of the 1940's World War II was raging and there were many privations that people suffered. Food, clothing and fuel were all rationed. This was generally accepted in good spirit. All families were encouraged to grow their own vegetables as well as "*make do & mend*" with clothing.

Most men were away in the war except for those in reserved occupations, medically unfit, too young or too old. There was no television: all news was from the wireless, newspapers, posters or on the "*Gaumont British Newsreel*" at the Pictures (cinema) but the community spirit was very high.

I look back on an idyllic childhood, we had such freedom. We could wander either alone or in small groups all over the hills, all around the area as well as inside the American Hospital Camps (even after dark!). We were never molested and didn't have any real fear of strangers. We were however very wary of "odd looking visitors" in case they were German spies! That included many of the scientists who descended on our domain to work at the then newly opened Telecommunications Research Establishment (TRE) now QinetiQ.

The village was a vibrant friendly community, we all knew our neighbours and looked after each other. Doors really didn't have to be locked, if they were the key was always found under the mat or on a string hanging behind the letter-box.

The local Bobby (policeman) knew everybody, he knew where to look if there were problems, and who's collar to feel!

The American GI's were very friendly and were generous to all the kids with plenty of gum, sweets and comics. We were all welcome to the camp Cinema. They also gave lavish - for the time - parties for the kids.

Food Rationing during World War II 1939 - 1945

(Some rationing carried on until 1954)

Quantities shown are per person per week

September 3rd 1939 - War was declared on Germany by Britain & France.

September 29th 1939 - National Register set up & Identity cards issued.

January 8th 1940 - Food rationing begins with 4oz. Butter, 12oz. Sugar & 4 oz. Bacon allowed a week per person. Petrol was also rationed.

March 1940 - 1s.10d worth of meat allowed per person a week (9p today). Sausages were not rationed but difficult to get; offal (liver, kidneys, tripe's) was originally un-rationed but sometimes formed part of the meat ration.

July 1940 - Tea 2oz 1s 10d (9p). Margarine, cooking fats and cheese rationed. Sugar cut to 8 oz 1s 10d (9p). The Government announced no more bananas no more fresh or tinned fruit to be imported except a few oranges for children only.

March 1941 - Jam, marmalade, treacle and syrup rationed. 8 oz /person/ week.

May 1941- Cheese ration increased to 2 oz's /person/week.

June 1941- Eggs: 1 fresh egg a week if available but often only one every two weeks. Meat ration cut to 1s 6d (7.5p) per person per week then to 1s 2d (6p): by June 1941 it was down to 1s (5p). Clothing rationing introduced with coupons issued.

July 1941- Sugar ration doubled to encourage people to make their own jam during the fruit season. Coal & Milk also went on ration

August 1941 - Extra cheese ration for manual workers.

December 1941 - Points scheme for food introduced. National dried milk introduced - Milk went on ration 3 pints (1800ml) per person per week occasionally dropping to 2 pints (1200ml). This amount also varied for young children and expectant mothers Expectant mothers children and invalids were allowed 7 pints of milk per week.

Expectant mothers and children were also allowed up to 18 eggs per month. Children were allowed orange and rosehip syrup as well as cod liver oil. Household milk (skimmed or dried) was available (1 packet per four weeks). Tea ration 2oz tea (9p) /person/week. Sugar cut to 8oz (9p) /person/week.

January 1942 Rice & Dried Fruit added to points system. Tea ration for under fives was withdrawn.
February 1942 Gas & Electricity rationed.

February 1942 Canned tomatoes and Peas. Soap rationed (1 small tablet each month).

April 1942 Breakfast cereals and condensed milk added to points system.

June 1942 - American dried egg powder on sale. 1s 9d (9p) per packet (equivalent to 12 eggs) Wholemeal loaf ("The National loaf") introduced (far more wheat used which meant less wastage). Sausages contained less and less real pork or beef. Horsemeat became more commonplace (later whale meat was also available).

July 1942 - Sweets and chocolate 2 oz per person per week.

August 1942 - Biscuits added to points system - Cheese ration was increased to 8 oz per person per week.

December 1942 Oat flakes added to points system.

1943 Sausages rationed.

December 1944 - Extra tea allowance for 70 year olds and over introduced.

January 1945 - Whale meat and Snoek (pike) introduced.

September 2nd 1945 WW II finally ended. Japanese surrender signed.

July 1946 - Bread was rationed (Yes - **after** the war ended!)

Dates Items Came off Ration

July 1948 - Bread.
December 1948 - Jam.
March 1949 - Clothing.
May 1950 - Points rationing ended. Petrol came off ration.
October 1952 - Tea.
February 1953 - Sweets.
April 1953 - Cream.
March 1953 - Eggs.
September 1953 - Sugar.
May 1954 - Butter, cheese, margarine, cooking fats & coal.
June 1954 - Meat and bacon.

The monthly food points system worked like this:-   The 16 points personal allowance per month let you to buy, for example:- One can of fish or meat, **or** 2lb (900g) of dried fruit, **or** 8lb (3.6kg) of split peas.   The Point system also included such food as condensed milk, rice and breakfast cereal. Points could be used to buy food anywhere, you didn't have to be registered as you did with ration books (coupons).

Clothing was also on a points system. Each person allowed sixty-six points a year, which was equal to one complete outfit of clothing for the average adult. Children's clothing had a lower Point value as they needed more replacements. As with food, the Points could be used anywhere.

Rationing continued for many years after the war ended, the last items came off ration as late as 1954, eight years after the end of the war. In spite of this I have no recollection of it being considered a great hardship. An inconvenience, yes! But it was accepted generally with a good grace, as everybody was affected the same.

There was, of course, a "black market" everywhere. Most items could be obtained if you knew the right people and/or were prepared to pay. The "Dad's Army" spiv really existed!

Befriend an American soldier and you never went short of anything (especially Nylon stockings if you were a girl!).

The Blackout (1939 - 1945)

Throughout the war there were no street lights, light must not show from any house at night-time. Every house had thick black-out curtains. Cars only had very dim shaded lights & all street names, place names, direction signs & mile-stones were either removed or obliterated. We all had to carry our gas-mask, in its case, wherever we went. We were bombarded with phrases such as *"Dig for Victory - grow more food"*, *"Careless talk costs lives"*, *"Coughs & sneezes spread diseases - trap your germs in your handkerchief"* etc. etc!

Most house and shop windows were given some blast protection from exploding bombs by criss-crossing the glass with sticky tape, some people went even further by sticking curtain net to the window panes with clear varnish. It made looking out of the window difficult. My parents did the latter, we had several holes scratched through the varnished netting to be able to peep out. It was wonderful at the end of the war to be able to clean it all off with razor blades and look out of the window properly once again.

The Utility kite mark

During and just after the war, materials of all sorts, including wood, clothing material, leather etc. were in very short supply. It was necessary to keep prices of essentials down but still of a durable quality. This resulted in everything - furniture, clothing, footwear etc. - being manufactured to a remarkably good, no frills, but durable, standard. It proved to be very functional, often still in service long after the war ended. Everything that passed this standard was marked with the official "Utility" kite mark.

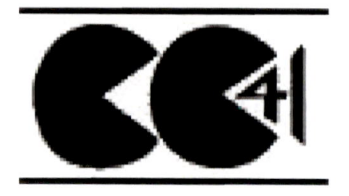

The official "Utility" kite mark, the 41 referred to 1941 when it was introduced.

The Utility scheme continued until 1952, 7 years after the war ended.

To make ends meet much clothing was home made by recycling old cloths.. It was common to unravel old knit-wear to re-use the wool.

A typical gasmask

A standard issue cardboard carrying case for one's gasmask

From time to time we had to have the masks tested and maybe have new filters fitted to protect against some new gas threat.

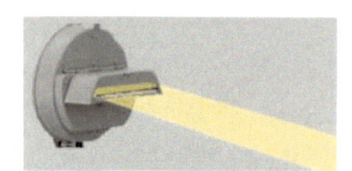

A typical headlight cover

A three slatted headlight cover

All vehicle headlights had to be masked so as to not be easily visible to enemy aircraft at night. The resulting light from the shielded headlamp was very poor indeed.

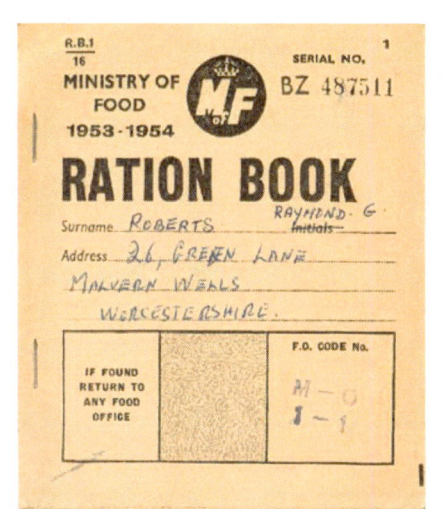

As children we were regularly measured and weighed, to see it we qualified for any extra rations of food or clothing..

Everybody had their own ration book, this was mine at the end of rationing. Its size was about 4.3" x 5" (110mm x 127mm)

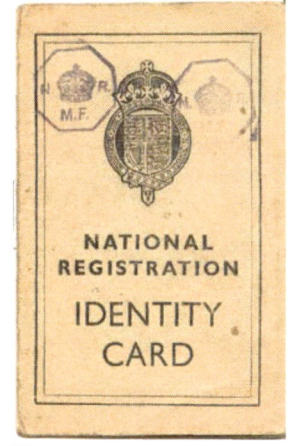

Every man, woman and child had an identity card like this.

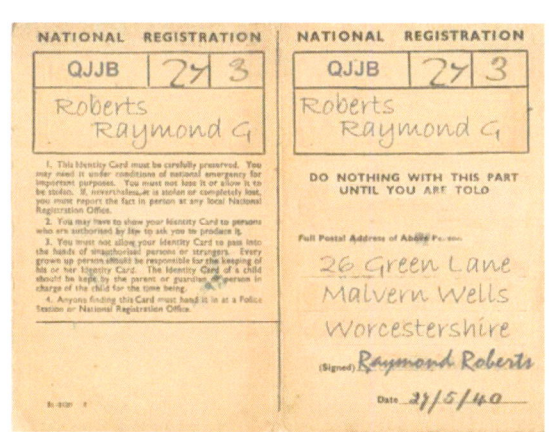

This was all the information the Identity Card contained. Its size was about 3.25" x 5" (83mm x 127mm) folded

Malvern Wells in the 1940's

[Map showing Malvern Wells village with labelled locations including: A449, Mr Hutton, Kings Road, Terminus, Hearts Bank, Back Road, Wood's Bakery, Warrington School, Charlie Hill's, The Quabbs, Village Hall, Jimmy Nurse's, Ernie Marsh's & Bert Richmond's, Cubs, Scouts, Guides, Brownies Etc., Village Institute, St. Peter's Church, The Dell, Cuffs, Wells House, The Wells Road, Thornbank School, Fire Station, Green Lane, Hornyold Rd, Cottage in the Wood, Daniels Garage, Essington Hotel, Hornyold Arms Hotel & Garage, Garret Theatre, Walker's Coals, Butcher's Pitch, Upper Welland, Brick Barns American Army Hospital Camp, North, Hanley Road, Cleeve Court Boys School, To Woodfarm American Army Hospital Camp, Wilson's Lane, Brick Barns Farm, Shuttlefast Lane, Sewage Farm, To Upton, To Malvern, Malvern Wells LMS Railway Station]

The Village of Malvern Wells in the 1940's

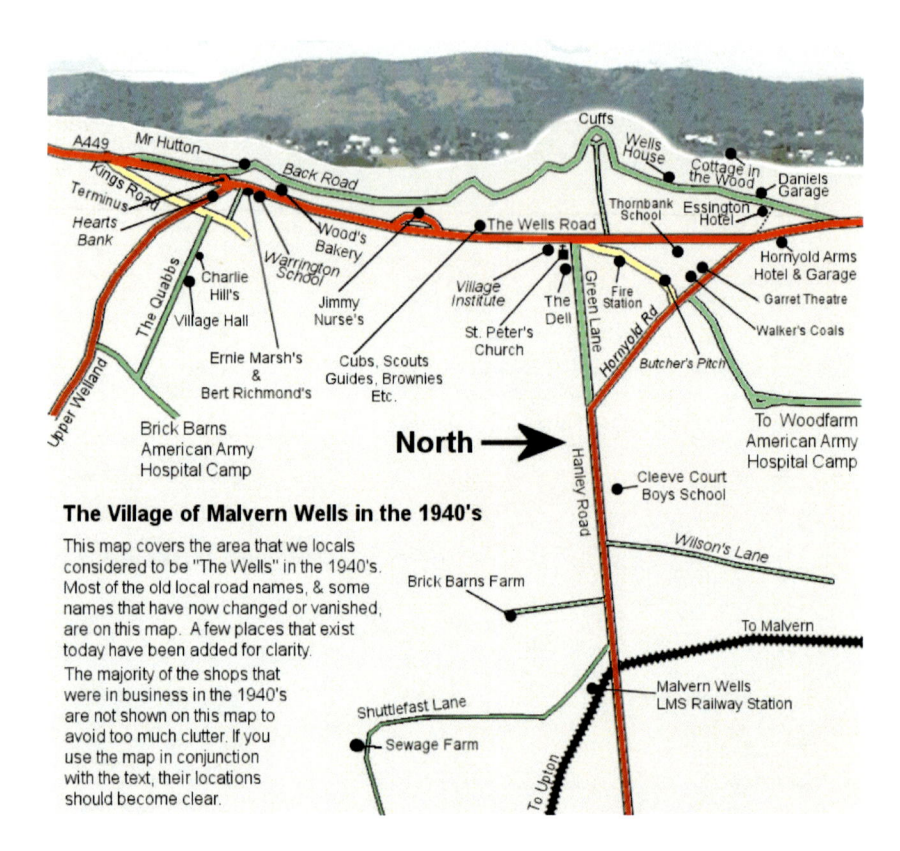

This map covers the area that we locals considered to be "The Wells" in the 1940's. Most of the old local road names, & some names that have now changed or vanished, are on this map. A few places that exist today have been added for clarity.

The majority of the shops that were in business in the 1940's are not shown on this map to avoid too much clutter. If you use the map in conjunction with the text, their locations should become clear.

*This shows the area that we locals considered "The Wells" in the 1940's
The street names above are the ones we used, as children, at that time*

Malvern Wells today

Of the nearly 70 'establishments' mentioned in this book, the only ones to survive in any way intact are the following:-

Warrington School still exists but has changed its name to *Malvern Wells C of E Primary School* and, as the name suggests, is now only a primary school.

The Abbey School still exists as a school, but has changed its name to *The Abbey College* and caters for foreign students from the age of 14 yrs.

The Working Mens Club has changed its name to *The Wells Club* but still exists in the same location.

The Village Institute still exists but with a slight name change to *The Village Hall*.

The red public telephone box still exists.

Holy Well, the bottling of pure "*Holywell Spring Water*" on site recommenced in December 2009

The Dell is one of only three businesses retaining both name and location.

The Cottage in the Wood is still trading exactly as it was then although much expanded.

Until recently there was a garage on the same spot as the **Hornyold Garage** known as Three Counties Services, this has now moved. The site is now the Wells Business Centre.

Holbrook's shop recently reopened as a general store, "*The 207 Store*", with the Post Office section as *Tailorbird Boutique*. Sadly "*The 207 Store*" has now closed, however *Tailorbird Boutique* has expanded to take over the entire shop space.

The American Army hospital camps, Brick Barn & Wood Farm, are now both Housing Developments.

Acknowledgments

Many old friends have helped me get the facts correct and I am particularly grateful for the help of all of the following:-.

Lil Roberts (nee Garbutt) Cousin by marriage. It was a chat with Lil on her 80th birthday that made us both realize that this information must be recorded whilst it is still possible to do so by the people who were there at the time. (Lil died 2 ½ years after that chat!)

Mary Addison (nee Young) Neighbour in the 40's

Derek Day, School friend

Peter Thomas   School friend

Hazel Cave (nee Drew), School friend

Barry Alison, School friend

John Hill, School friend

Doreen Davies (nee Jeynes), family friend (claims to have bounced me on her knee when I was a baby)

Stan Pratty, School friend

Elizabeth Jeffes, Daughter of Ron Jeffes the Chemist.